Wonders

FLORIDA

Reading/Writing Companion

McGraw Hill

ABOUT THE COVER

Aquariums

Look! It is a green sea turtle. It gets its name from the green fat under its shell. What makes it green? The green sea plants the turtle eats! To find food, the sea turtle uses its strong flippers to swim. The sea turtle uses its sharp jaws to tear the plants it eats.

Some green sea turtles live at aquariums. You can find many aquariums in Florida. Aquariums are places that help to rescue and protect many animals and plants. These living things all live in or around water. You can see dolphins and penguins. You can see corals and many kinds of colorful fish. Sometimes they see you, too!

mheducation.com/prek-12

Mc Graw Hill

Send all inquiries to:
McGraw Hill
1325 Avenue of the Americas
New York, NY 10019

ISBN: 978-0-07-700915-1
MHID: 0-07-700915-0

Printed in the United States of America.

5 6 7 8 9 10 11 SWI 26 25 24 23 22

B

Welcome to FLORIDA WONDERS!

We are so excited about how much you will learn and grow this year! We're here to help you set goals for your learning.

You will explore new ideas by reading different texts.

Each week, we will set goals on the My Goals page. Here is an example:

I can read and understand texts.

As you read and write, you will learn skills and strategies to help you reach your goals.

You will think about your learning and sometimes circle a hand to show your progress.

Here are some questions you can ask yourself.

- Did I understand the task?
- Was it easy?
- Was it hard?
- What made it hard?

If you need more help, you can choose what to do.

- Talk to a friend or teacher.
- Use an Anchor Chart.
- Choose a center activity.

At the end of each week, you will complete a fun task to show what you have learned.

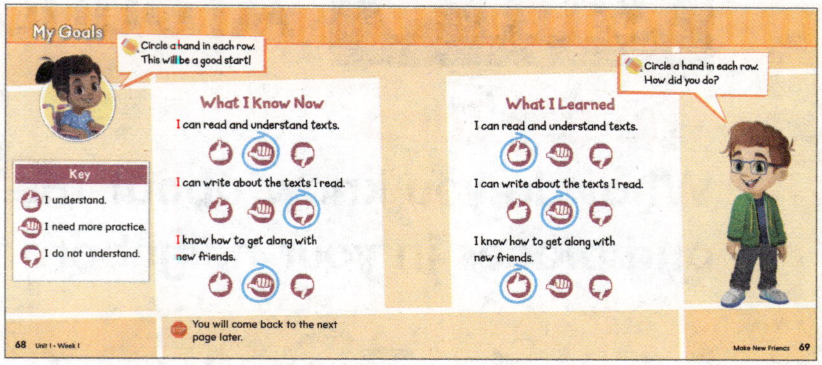

Then you will return to your My Goals page and think about your learning.

Unit 4 Around the Neighborhood

The Big Idea

Week 1 • Time for Work

Digital Tools *Find this eBook and other resources at:* my.mheducation.com

ML Harris/Iconica/Getty Images

Week 2 • Meet Your Neighbors

Week 3 • Pitch In

Extended Writing

Personal Narrative

Connect and Reflect

Purestock/SuperStock

Unit 4

Around the Neighborhood

The Big Idea

What do you know about the people and places in your neighborhood?

Talk about what the neighbors in the picture are doing.

Circle the neighbors who are playing together.

Post Office
Grocery
STOP
U.S. Mail

Build Knowledge

Essential Question What do people use to do their jobs?

Build Vocabulary

Talk about things people use to do their jobs. What are some words that name these things?

Draw a picture of one of these things.

Write the word.

Tanya Constantine/Blend Images/Getty Images

My Goals

Circle a hand in each row.
It will be fun to learn more.

Key

I understand.

I need more practice.

I do not understand.

What I Know Now

I can read and understand texts.

I can write about the texts I read.

I know what people use to do their jobs.

STOP You will come back to the next page later.

Circle a hand in each row.
What are you getting better at?

What I Learned

I can read and understand texts.

I can write about the texts I read.

I know what people use to do their jobs.

Retell the nonfiction text.

Write about the text.

An important fact I learned is

Text Evidence
Page

An interesting part of the text is

Text Evidence
Page

Talk about special clothing that workers wear.

Draw and **write** about a worker who wears special clothes.

This worker wears

Reread **Big Book**

Details in the words and photos in a nonfiction text give information about the **topic**.

Listen to and **look** at part of the text.

Talk about the topic and details.

Write two details.

Two details are

____

1. ______________________________

____

2. ______________________________

Draw one detail you wrote about.

Talk about how the words and photos help you learn information.

Check In

Reread Big Book

Listen to and look at pages 13–18.

Talk about how each question has an answer.

Draw the answer to the question on page 13.

Look at pages 25–30.

Talk about how the author shows that each shoe goes with a worker.

Draw and **write** about a shoe from the text.

This shoe is good because

Find Text Evidence

Read to find out about a firehouse.

Circle and read the word **you**.

Tom On Top!

Susan Kuklin/Photo Researchers/Getty Images

Can you see a  ?

firehouse

stevegeer/iStock/Getty Images

Shared Read

Find Text Evidence

Ask questions you may have about the text as you read. This can help you learn information.

Read each sentence. Point to and name the first letter and end mark in each sentence.

I can see a .
fire truck

Richard Semik/Alamy

I can see a  firefighter.

ML Harris/Iconica/Getty Images

Shared Read

Find Text Evidence

Circle what is red on page 22.

Underline the lowercase letters on page 23.

I can see a hose.

I can see a  hat.

Ted Horowitz/Alamy

Shared Read

Find Text Evidence

Circle words that have the same middle sound as **mop**.

Retell the text. Use the words and photos to help you.

Richard Hutchings/Photo Researchers/Getty Images

I can see Tom on top!

Reread

Paired Selection

Look at the photos. What tools do firefighters use?

Talk about the tools you see in the big and little photos.

Draw a line from the tool in the little photo to the same tool in the big photo.

hose

boots

helmet

Quick Tip

You can use these sentence starters:

Firefighters ____.

They use ____.

Talk about the tools in the little photos. Choose one to write about.

Write how this tool helps firefighters.

This tool is

____

This tool helps firefighters

____

____

Talk About It

Why does the author include photos and labels?

Workers and Their Tools

Step 1 **Talk** about jobs and the tools workers use. Choose a job.

Step 2 **Write** a question about the tools a worker needs to do that job.

Step 3 **Look** at books or use the Internet. You can also talk with a worker who does that job.

Step 4 **Draw** and **write** about what you learned.

Step 5 **Choose** a good way to present your work.

Make Connections

Talk about what this worker is doing. What tools is he using?

Compare these tools to the tools you read about in other texts this week.

Quick Tip

You can use these sentence starters:

The worker is ___.

Tools from other texts are ___.

syolacan/E+/Getty Images

Show Your Knowledge

Write About a Job

1. **Think** about the texts you read. What did you learn about things people use to do their jobs?

2. **Choose** two jobs that you read about. **Draw** the workers and the things they need to do their jobs.

3. **Write** about what would happen if the workers traded their tools. Use words that you learned this week.

Build Knowledge

Essential Question Who are your neighbors?

Build Vocabulary

SOCIAL STUDIES

Talk about who your neighbors are. What are some words that name different neighbors?

Draw a picture of a neighbor.

Write the word.

My Goals

Circle a hand in each row. Whatever you know is okay!

Key

I understand.

I need more practice.

I do not understand.

What I Know Now

I can read and understand texts.

I can write about the texts I read.

I know who my neighbors are.

STOP You will come back to the next page later.

Circle a hand in each row.
It is okay if you need more practice.

What I Learned

I can read and understand texts.

I can write about the texts I read.

I know who my neighbors are.

Read

Respond to the Big Book

Retell the realistic fiction story.

Write about the story.

A paleta is good because

Text Evidence

Page

This is realistic fiction because

Text Evidence

Page

Talk about what the girl, her family, and her neighbors do with a paleta.

Draw and **write** about what you would do with a paleta.

I would

Reread **Big Book**

The main character is who a fiction story is mostly about. The setting is where the story takes place.

Listen to and look at the story.

Talk about the main character and the setting.

Write about the main character.

The main character is

____

____

____

Draw and **write** about the setting.

The neighborhood is

Check In

Reread **Big Book**

Listen to and **look** at page 27.

Talk about how the girl's words help you see, feel, and smell the roses.

Draw and **write** about the roses. Use words from the story to help you.

The roses are

Listen to and **look** at pages 27–31.

Draw and **write** about the character who is telling the story. What might she say about where she lives?

I like where I live because

Shared Read

Find Text Evidence

Ask questions you may have before reading the story. Then read to find the answers.

Circle and read the word **Do**.

Sid

Do Sid and Mom like it?

Shared Read

Find Text Evidence

Circle an object on this page whose name begins with the same sound as **dip**.

Underline words that tell what Dan can do.

Sid and Mom do like it!

Dan can tap, tap on a  door.

Shared Read

Find Text Evidence

Circle the picture of Dot on page 46.

Underline words on page 47 that begin with the same sound as **did**.

Dot can tap, tap on a  door.

Dot and Dan can sip.

Shared Read

Find Text Evidence

Circle words that end with the same sound as sad.

Retell the story. Use the words and pictures to help you.

Tod can tap, tap on a .
door

Sid and Tod pat a 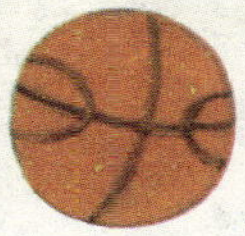 .

ball

Reread

Paired Selection

Listen to pages 33–35.

Quick Tip

You can use these sentence starters:

The name of the character is ___.

One of the places he goes is ___.

Circle the character in the picture who is telling the story.

Write his name. Tell what he likes to do.

Talk about the places where Caleb goes in his neighborhood.

Draw a place where Caleb goes. Show what he does there.

Write About It

Caleb wrote a personal narrative about himself and what he likes to do. Now write about yourself and what you like to do.

Neighbors Interview

Step 1 **Talk** about different things neighbors do together.

Step 2 **Write** a question about things neighbors do together.

Step 3 **Ask** classmates and neighbors your question.

Step 4 **Draw** what you learned.

Step 5 **Choose** a good way to present your work.

Integrate

Make Connections

Talk about what these neighbors are doing together. How are they having fun?

Compare these neighbors to the neighbors in *What Can You Do with a Paleta?*

Quick Tip

You can use these sentence starters:

These neighbors are ___.

The neighbors in the story are ___.

kali9/E+/Getty Images

Show Your Knowledge

Make a Neighbor Book

1. **Think** about the texts you read. What did you learn about neighbors?
2. **Talk** to a neighbor. **Draw** two things you learned about your neighbor.
3. **Write** words that tell about your pictures. Use words that you learned this week.

Think about what you learned this week.
Turn to page 35.

Build Knowledge

Essential Question **How can people help to make their community better?**

Build Vocabulary

Talk about how people can help make their community better. What words tell about how people can help?

Draw a picture of one of the words.

Write the word.

My Goals

Circle a hand in each row.
It is important to do your best.

Key

I understand.

I need more practice.

I do not understand.

What I Know Now

I can read and understand texts.

I can write about the texts I read.

I know how people can help make my community better.

STOP You will come back to the next page later.

Circle a hand in each row. Keep up the good work!

What I Learned

I can read and understand texts.

I can write about the texts I read.

I know how people can help make my community better.

Read

Respond to the Big Book

Retell the nonfiction text.

Write about the text.

An interesting fact I learned is

Text Evidence

Page

I know this text is nonfiction because

Text Evidence

Page

Talk about workers who help your community.

Draw a worker who helps.

Share how the worker you drew helps your community.

Reread **Big Book**

Details give us information about the order of events, or time order, in a text. The words *first, next,* and *last* tell the order.

Listen to and look at part of the text.

Talk about what happens *first, next,* and *last.*

Draw what happens.

First

Next

Last

Check In

Reread **Big Book**

Listen to and **look** at pages 14–15.

Talk about the sound words the author uses. How do these words help you know what the workers are doing?

Write your ideas.

The words help me know

Listen to and **look** at page 32.
Why do you think the author added this page?

Talk about the different machines and facts about them.

Draw one of the machines.
Show a fact about it.

Shared Read

Find Text Evidence

Ask questions about the story before you read. Then read to find out what the mom and girl can do.

Circle and read the words **and, go,** and **to**.

I Can, You Can!

Mom and I go to a .
beach

Shared Read

Find Text Evidence

Circle what the girl can pat, pat, pat.

Underline and read the word **you**.

I can pat, pat, pat on top.

Can you pat it?

Shared Read

Find Text Evidence

Circle the picture of Stan.

Underline the word that begins with the same sounds as **spin**.

I can tip, tip it on top.

Stan can spot it.

Shared Read

Find Text Evidence

Circle the word that begins with the same sounds as snip.

Retell the story. Use the words and pictures to help you.

I can pat, pat, pat on top.

We can do it in a snap!

Reread Paired Selection

Look at the photos. How can people work together to plant a garden?

First they dig. Next they plant seeds. Then they water.

Talk about the words that help you know the order of each step.

Circle the words that tell the order.

SOCIAL STUDIES

Listen to page 36.

Talk about what happens when the vegetables are ready to pick.

Write what happens last.

Last

____

____

Talk About It

Talk about ways people can help make a garden. How can a garden help a community?

Neil Guegan/Image Source

Interview About School

Step 1 **Talk** about ways you can make your school community better.

Step 2 **Write** a question about things you can do to help your school.

Step 3 **Ask** classmates and school workers your question.

Step 4 **Draw** and **write** about what you learned.

We can make our school better by

Step 5 **Choose** a good way to present your work.

Make Connections

Talk about how these people pitch in to help their community.

Compare how these people help their community to how the workers in *Roadwork* help their community.

Quick Tip

You can use these sentence starters:

These people help by ___.

The people in the text help by ___.

These people donate clothing and other items to people who need them.

Make a Community Quilt

1. **Think** about the texts you read. What did you learn about how you can help make your community better?

2. **Make** a quilt square. **Draw** one way you can make your community better.

3. **Write** about the way you can make it better. Use words that you learned this week.

Writing and Grammar

I wrote a personal narrative. It is a story that tells about something that happened to me.

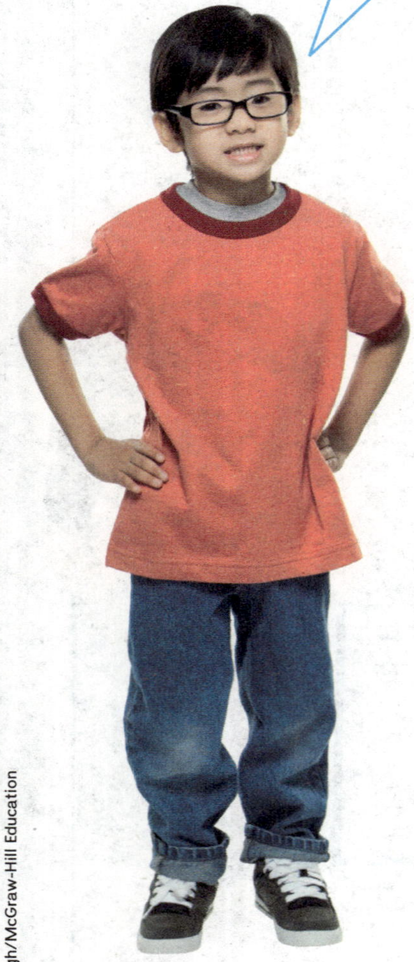

Yoshi

Ken Cavanagh/McGraw-Hill Education

Personal Narrative

My personal narrative tells about an event that was special to me.

Student Model

My Mystery Trip

My Uncle Shiro took me to the airport.

But we did not get on a plane.

We watched gigantic jets land and take off.

It was loud.

I had so much fun!

Genre Study

Talk about what makes Yoshi's writing a personal narrative.

Ask any questions you have about personal narratives.

Circle how Yoshi feels about the trip.

Writing and Grammar

Plan

Talk about something that happened to you.

Draw what happened.

Quick Tip

Think of an event that was special to you.

Write what your personal narrative is about.

My personal narrative is about

Draw a detail that happened.

Writing and Grammar

Draft

Read Yoshi's draft of his personal narrative.

Quick Tip

Remember: A **draft** is the first writing we do. We organize our first ideas in a draft.

Student Model

A Trip to the Airport

My Uncle Shiro took me to the airport.
But we did not get on a plane.
We watched jets.
I had so much fun!

Time Order
I put the events in order.

I included a detail that tells more about what happened.

Writing Skill
I used my Word Bank to help me spell this word.

Your Turn

Begin to write your personal narrative in your writer's notebook. Use your ideas from pages 82-83.

Writing and Grammar

Revise and Edit

Think about how Yoshi revised and edited his personal narrative.

Student Model

My Mystery Trip

My Uncle Shiro took me to the airport.

But we did not get on a plane.

We watched gigantic jets land and take off.

It was loud.

I had so much fun!

I wrote a better title.

I made sure to spell the word *the* correctly.

I added a **sentence**. It tells a complete idea.

I added an **adjective**.

I added details to make my writing more interesting.

Grammar

- A **sentence** is a group of words that tells a complete idea.
- An **adjective,** or describing word, tells more about a noun.

I added more details to my picture.

Your Turn

Revise and edit your personal narrative. Be sure to use complete sentences and adjectives. Use your checklist.

Share and Evaluate

Practice presenting your work with a partner. Take turns.

Present your work. Then use this checklist.

Review Your Work	Yes	No
Writing		
I wrote a personal narrative.	☐	☐
I added details.	☐	☐
I used my Word Bank to help spell words.	☐	☐
Speaking and Listening		
I spoke in a loud, clear voice.	☐	☐
I asked questions.	☐	☐

Talk with a partner about your writing.

Write about your work.

What did you do well in your writing?

What do you need to work on?

Find Out About Firefighters

Listen to "Firefighters Help Out!"

Talk about different jobs firefighters do.

Draw one job that a firefighter does.

Purestock/SuperStock

Compare the ways firefighters help in a community.

Write about one way they help.

Quick Tip

You can use these sentence starters:

One way firefighters help is ____.

Another way they help is ____.

Firefighters help by

Make a Job Poster

Talk about different jobs people do and the tools they use.

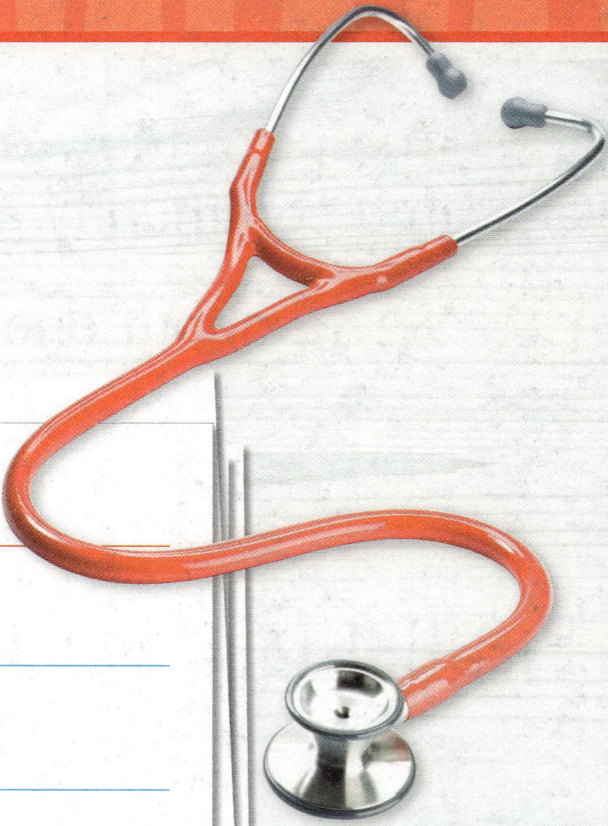

What to Do

1. **Draw** a job that people do.
   Show the tools the worker uses.
2. **Add** details to your poster.
3. **Write** a caption for your poster.
4. **Share** and compare your poster.

You Need

pencil

crayons

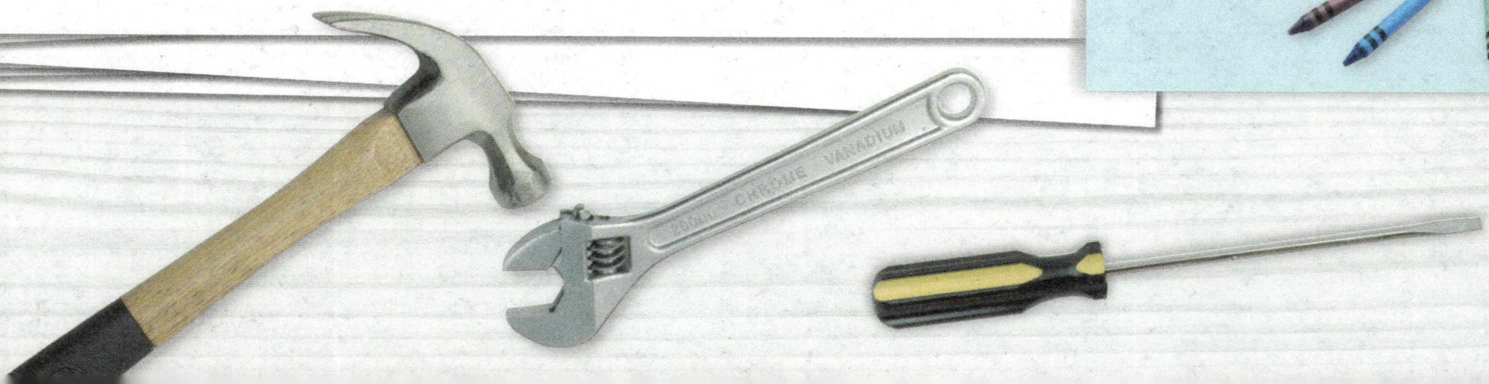

Extend Your Learning

Choose Your Own Book

Minutes I Read

Write the title of the book.

Tell a partner why you want to read it.
Then read the book.

Write your opinion of the book.

Think About Your Learning

Think about what you learned in this unit.

Share one thing you did well.

Write one thing you want to get better at.

My Sound-Spellings

Aa

a
apple

Bb

b
bat

Cc

c ck k
camel

Dd

d
dolphin

Ee

e
egg

Ff

f
fire

Gg

g
guitar

Hh

h_
hippo

Ii

i
insect

Jj

j
jump

Kk

c k ck
koala

Ll

l
lemon

Mm

m
map

Nn

n
nest

Oo

o
octopus

Pp

p
piano

Qq

qu_
queen

Rr

r
rose

Ss

s
sun

Tt

t
turtle

Uu

u
umbrella

Vv

v
volcano

Ww

w_
window

Xx

x
box

Yy

y_
yo-yo

Zz

z
_s
zipper

Credits: (apple) Stockdisc/PunchStock; (bat) Radlund & Associates/Artville/Getty Images; (camel) Photodisc/Getty Images; (dolphin) Arco Images/Petra Wegner/imageBROKER/Alamy; (egg) Pixtal/age fotostock; (fire) Comstock Images/Alamy; (guitar) Jules Frazier/Photodisc Green/Getty Images; (hippo) Michele Burgess/Corbis; (insect) Photodisc/Getty Images; (jump) Rubberball Productions/Getty Images; (koala) Al Franklin/Corbis; (lemon) C Squared Studios/Getty Images; (map) McGraw-Hill Education; (nest) Siede Preis/Photodisc/Getty Images; (octopus) Photographers Choice RF/SuperStock; (piano) Photo Spin/Artville/Alamy Stock Photo; (queen) Joshua Ets-Hokin/Photodisc/Getty Images; (rose) Steve Cole/Photodisc/Getty Images; (sun) 97/E+/Getty Images; (turtle) Ingram Publishing; (umbrella) Stockbyte/Punchstock/Getty Images; (volcano) Westend61/Getty Images; (window) Photodisc/Getty Images; (box) C Squared Studios/Photodisc/Getty Images; (yo-yo) D. Hurst/Alamy; (zipper) Matthew Cant/ImageState/Alamy.

Handwriting Models

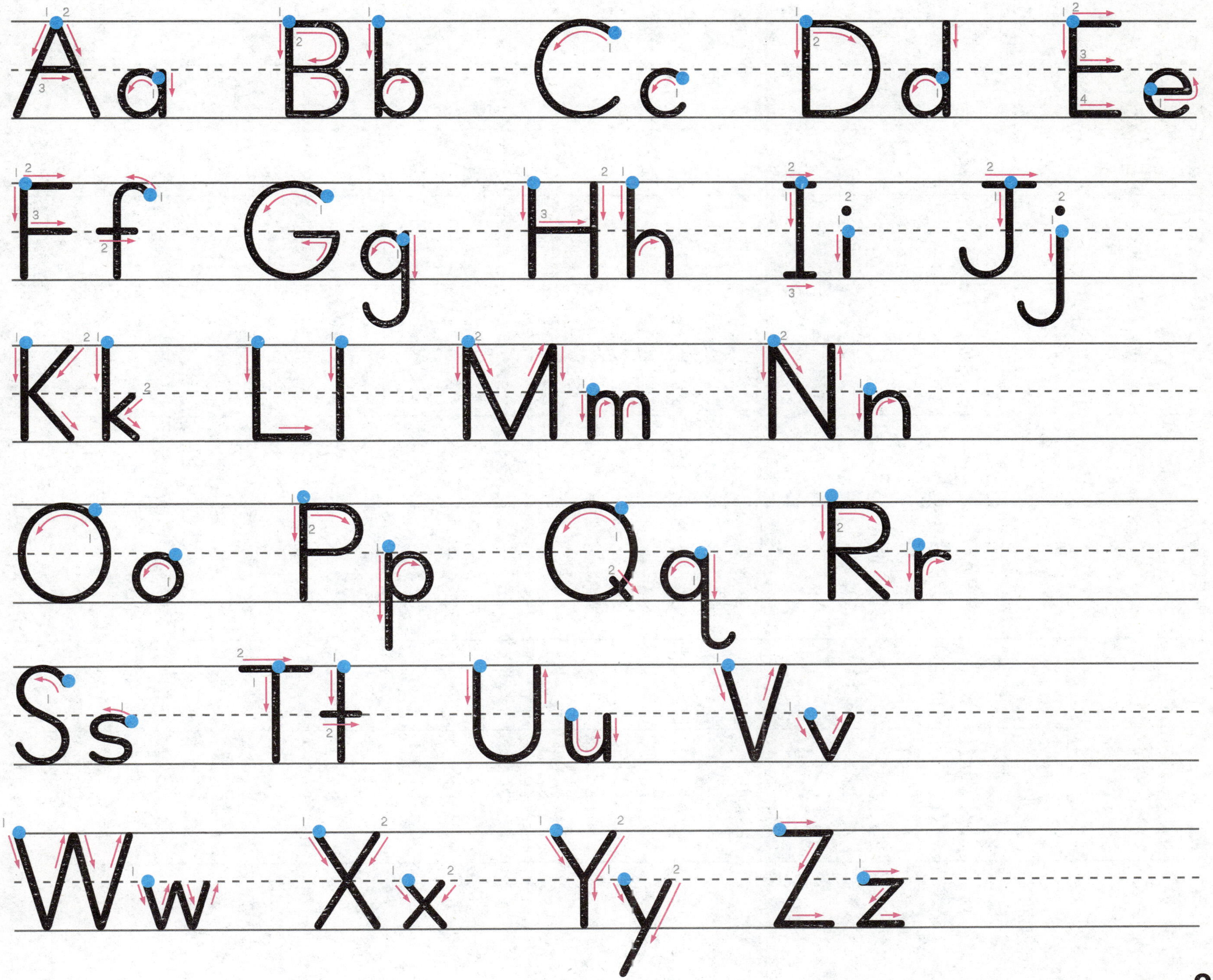